Marcelo Paulo Stracke
Priscila P. Martins

Management of industrial liquid effluent with potential for utilisation

AF671658

Marcelo Paulo Stracke
Priscila P. Martins

Management of industrial liquid effluent with potential for utilisation

ScienciaScripts

Imprint

Any brand names and product names mentioned in this book are subject to trademark, brand or patent protection and are trademarks or registered trademarks of their respective holders. The use of brand names, product names, common names, trade names, product descriptions etc. even without a particular marking in this work is in no way to be construed to mean that such names may be regarded as unrestricted in respect of trademark and brand protection legislation and could thus be used by anyone.

Cover image: www.ingimage.com

This book is a translation from the original published under ISBN 978-3-330-75310-5.

Publisher:
Sciencia Scripts
is a trademark of
Dodo Books Indian Ocean Ltd. and OmniScriptum S.R.L publishing group

120 High Road, East Finchley, London, N2 9ED, United Kingdom
Str. Armeneasca 28/1, office 1, Chisinau MD-2012, Republic of Moldova, Europe
Printed at: see last page
ISBN: 978-620-8-09516-1

Copyright © Marcelo Paulo Stracke, Priscila P. Martins
Copyright © 2024 Dodo Books Indian Ocean Ltd. and OmniScriptum S.R.L publishing group

Chapter 1 INTRODUCTION

Due to the great movement that environmental/environmental management has generated in companies, which is fundamental to the success or failure of a company, various measures are being taken in organisations to ensure effective management; in addition to adopting strategies and seeking certifications, many are aware of the need to invest in environmentally oriented projects.

The investigation is being carried out at the company Gama SA in Santo Ângelo, which produces and distributes beverages under The Coca-Cola Company brand and covers the entire state of Rio Grande do Sul and Santa Catarina.

Environmental management is an issue that the vast majority of companies are concerned with. There are companies that use this attitude to develop their product marketing and others that are really concerned with developing activities to protect the environment.

Corporate responsibility for the environment is the result of interaction with factors both outside the organisation (authorities, regulatory bodies, environmental movement) and inside the organisation (safety and environment department, research and development department, quality department and production department).

In Brazil, there are laws and regulations that govern environmental management, as well as ISO 14000, an international standard that promotes the elements of an effective environmental management system that can be integrated into other organisations, where companies seek continuous improvement; reduction of implementation costs; certifications; improvement and customer satisfaction; optimisation of the company's infrastructure and personnel, and the demand for and consumption of products that comply with environmental standards is gradually increasing. For this reason, it is not possible to treat environmental issues as a matter external to organisations. Analysing environmental costs has become an eminent necessity due to the demands of the market and is therefore a prerequisite for competitiveness.

By investing in environmental issues, the company can reduce additional costs such as losses and fines for activities that damage the environment. It is not enough for a company to decide to invest in environmental issues without implementing an environmental management system, because for this to be effective, the procedures must be carried out as part of a structured management system that is integrated into the company's general management activities.

Finally, this study within the environmental system aims to verify the feasibility of using the purified wastewater for fertilisation through technical reports, so that we can analyse the conditions and quality of the water and reuse it for application in a vegetable crop to support the growth and development of the plant.

1.1 Objectives

1.1.1 General information:

- Check the feasibility of using liquid wastewater for fertilisation on the basis of technical reports.

1.1.2 Specific:

- Investigate the environmental management applied in the factory to assess the feasibility of using liquid effluent for fertilisation;

- Learn about the fertilisation process used in agriculture to investigate the feasibility of using liquid wastewater for fertilisation;

- Analysis of the chemical parameters of the treated wastewater to determine whether it can be used for the fertilisation process in order to conduct a feasibility study on the use of liquid wastewater for fertilisation;Study of the nutrients needed for plant growth and enrichment to investigate the feasibility of using liquid wastewater for fertilisation;

- Monitoring the wastewater treatment process at the Gama SA wastewater treatment plant to investigate the feasibility of using the liquid wastewater for fertilisation.

1.2 Justification

In view of its limited availability and increasing demand, water should be regarded as an economic good and an indispensable commodity for life, which is involved in essential ecological processes and serves as a habitat and ecological niche for countless organisms, animal and plant species. Its mobility, its solubility, its fluctuations in density, its property as a heat regulator and, above all, its surface tension are attributes that justify its ecological function.

This work is therefore justified in order to support the company in the reuse of the water from the wastewater treated by the fertilisation process, thus constantly improving its environmental management system and minimising possible environmental impacts by looking for alternatives for the correct treatment of this precious liquid after its use in the industrial process, in order to be able to return it to the environment in the best possible way, since the presence of water in the environment guarantees the continuity of life.

Chapter 2 THEORETICAL BACKGROUND

To be able to work in a company in the environmental field, it is not enough to specialise in this subject, but one must be aware that nowadays it is important to know new ways to reuse the available resources, to promote them at all levels of industrial activity and to always look for ways to control and minimise the environmental impact that may occur during the production process - facts that were not given so much importance in the past, but which today are an important differentiator in the highly competitive labour market and in the environment.

> "When the last tree has fallen, when the last river has dried up, when the last fish has been caught, you will realise that money cannot be eaten" (GREENPEACE).

In the past, those in charge at companies were only concerned with maintaining the production process without thinking about the environment, perhaps because they thought that nature's resources would never run out.

At a certain point, however, parts of society and the organisations themselves became aware of the environmental problem, as Donaire mentions:

> Originally, companies only had to worry about the efficiency of production systems. Until a certain point in time in the 1960s, this was the prevailing mentality in management practice and reflected the idea of unlimited markets and resources. In a short time, this notion proved to be wrong, as it became clear that the environment in which companies operate is becoming increasingly complex and that the decision-making process is subject to ever greater constraints. An important component of this shift in thinking and behaviour was the growing ecological awareness in society, in government and in the companies themselves, which began to incorporate this orientation into their strategies. The effects of this revolution can be seen in the change of emphasis in management theory: Authors began to explore new concepts (1999, p. 11).

In the course of the globalisation of the economy and the internationalisation of markets, entrepreneurs were not only concerned with the growth of their company and its favourable financial situation, but also with the environment, as natural resources and raw materials were becoming increasingly scarce and their waste products were increasingly polluting the environment.

According to Donaire, it is known that,

> The environment is increasingly becoming a mandatory item on the agenda of company managers. The globalisation of the economy, the internationalisation of the

> environmental quality standards described in the ISO 14000 series, the growing awareness of today's consumers and the spread of environmental education in schools indicate that the demands of future consumers for the preservation of the environment and quality of life will increase. In view of this, organisations must include the environmental variable in their scenario planning and decision-making and adopt a responsible attitude towards environmental issues.

According to Miranda (2011), the awakening of environmental awareness stems from people realising that they live on a planet whose natural resources are finite. The ongoing global crisis has led to a scarcity of some of these resources as natural resources continue to be depleted and the pursuit of development and high technology has had a negative impact. Responsible, environmentally friendly behaviour in terms of sustainable development using new technologies is now a matter of survival, a requirement with a sense of responsibility for the future of our planet and future generations.

Business organisations and their managers who are not yet aware of the importance of environmental protection should be made aware of the need to review and formulate their policies and plans on this issue, as business decisions to protect and preserve the environment are fast becoming indispensable conditions for significant business operations (MIRANDA, 2011).

However, according to Donaire (1999), an environmental management programme must be comprehensively discussed and analysed before it is implemented so that the best decision can be made.

> Organisations that want to harmonise their development with environmental issues must include an appropriate environmental management programme in their strategic and operational planning so that the environmental objectives are compatible with the organisation's other objectives. Environmental management programmes define the activities to be carried out, their sequence and the persons responsible for their implementation. As a rule, they should cover the most important environmental aspects and aim for continuous improvement by expanding their scope over time. They must be dynamic and flexible enough to adapt to changes that may occur both in their immediate environment and in the future (DONAIRE, 1999, p. 108).

Environmental management is becoming an important management tool for training and creating competitive conditions for companies, regardless of their economic segment, as change and the ecological impact on the economy will be felt ever more strongly and with ever more profound economic effects, since organisations that make strategic decisions that incorporate ecological environmental issues will achieve significant competitive advantages when it comes to reducing costs and increasing profits in the medium and long term (DONAIRE, 1999).

Therefore, the introduction of environmental management is important for a company for several reasons. Firstly, because it associates its image with the protection of the environment, thus improving the brand image of its products on the market. Companies that adopt this system are able to reduce their costs by avoiding waste and reusing previously discarded materials (MIRANDA, 2011).

According to Dias (2006), this new reality implies a radical change in the attitude of private and public organisations in the business world, which are increasingly taking public opinion on environmental issues into account. It can therefore be said that people are increasingly concerned about the quality of life in all respects, especially in relation to environmental issues, and that they favour products from environmentally conscious companies. In this sense, it is obvious that companies that do not meet these requirements are jeopardising their global competitiveness.

The introduction of the environmental management process is one of the reactions of companies to these pressures. Donaire (1999, p.23) cites:

> The concern of many organisations about the problem of pollution has led them to re-evaluate their production processes and look for cleaner technologies and the reuse of waste. This has led to significant savings that would not have been realised if they had not addressed this issue.

As a result, many organisations have gradually begun to incorporate the environmental dimension into their corporate management. In this context, Donaire (1999) emphasises the economic and strategic benefits of environmental management processes in companies.

According to the author mentioned above, the economic advantages are as follows:

1. Cost savings
    - Savings due to lower consumption of water, energy and other operating resources;
    - Savings through recycling, sale and utilisation of waste and reduction of waste water;
    - Reduction of fines and penalties for environmental pollution.

2. Higher income
    - Increasing the marginal contribution of "green products" that can be sold at higher prices;
    - Higher market share due to product innovations and less competition;
    - New product lines for new markets.

3. Strategic advantages
    - Improvement of the institutional image;
    - Renewal of the product portfolio;
    - Increased productivity;
    - High level of employee commitment;
    - Improved labour relations;
    - Improvement and creativity for new challenges;
    - Improved relations with environmental authorities, the community and environmental groups;
    - Better compliance with environmental standards.

If a company needs to apply for environmental certification in the near future, a "game of costs and benefits" will certainly begin, which must be well known in order to allow an effective evaluation of the concept of environmental quality (ALBERTI, 2000). However, despite the implementation of an environmental management system by some companies in Brazil, environmental quality is still considered a cost factor, although many companies are already reaping the benefits and high profitability.

When introducing an environmental management system, the organisation must allocate resources such as human, financial and technical resources, which initially involves additional effort and costs for adapting the system. The control of documentation and information related to environmental quality requirements is defined by the system and then determined by the standard itself and the policy established by the organisation.

If the system is well implemented and efficiently monitored and continuous improvement is pursued, a number of other important points can be highlighted, such as the reduction of implementation costs, certifications, audits and the maintenance of environmental management systems, the improvement of internal and external customer satisfaction, the optimisation of the company's infrastructure and personnel, and the benefits for the company, employees and the community.

The environmental responsibility of companies is the result of the interaction of factors outside the organisation (authorities, supervisory bodies, environmental movement) and inside the organisation (safety and environmental department, research and development, quality and production).

According to Donaire (1999), organisations need to consider the following steps for successful environmental management to avoid making too many mistakes and failing the plan: Develop and publish an environmental policy; set objectives and continually evaluate results; clearly define the environmental responsibilities of each division and administrative staff; disseminate the policy, goals and objectives and responsibilities internally and externally; obtain adequate resources; train and educate staff and inform consumers and the community; follow the evolution of the debate on environmental issues; participate in community environmental programmes and invest in research and development related to environmental areas; help balance the different interests of all stakeholders: business, consumers, society, shareholders and others.

2.1 Environmental management system

A very important issue that concerns nations around the world and all companies in every sector is the preservation of the environment. The ISO 14000 series of standards was created to support this concern.

This standard is based on two other systems: the British standard BS 7750 (which was originally only developed for companies of this origin) and the European Union's eco-management system.

The ISO 14001 series is an internationally recognised standard that specifies the requirements for the establishment and operation of an environmental management system. An environmental management system (EMS) is a framework developed to enable an organisation to consistently control its significant environmental impacts and continuously improve its operations and business (WHAT..., n.d.).

ISO 14001 is a tool to ensure efficient and effective management of environmental issues and impacts and to fulfil legal requirements. It is a standard with basic guidelines for the development of an environmental management system. The standard is part of ABNT NBR ISO 14000, the designation for a family of rules that also includes ISO 14001. This family specifies the requirements for an environmental management system and enables an organisation or company to develop and implement environmentally sound strategies and objectives. It also takes into account environmental aspects that are influenced by the organisation and others that it can control. The implementation of ISO 14001 should be sought by companies wishing to implement or improve an environmental management system, verify their environmental policy or demonstrate their compliance with sustainable practices to customers and external organisations. The application of the standard depends on factors such as the organisation's environmental policy, the nature of its activities, its products and services, the locations and the conditions under which the system operates (WHAT..., n.d.; SYSTEMS..., n.d.).

The introduction of the ISO 14001 standard in the country has helped to strengthen the concept of sustainability. Companies have begun to take initiatives that encompass both environmental quality and corporate social responsibility, as well as health and safety in the workplace. In this way, correct socio-ecological practices have become widespread in the business sector. Today, the implementation of ISO 14001 is an indisputable sign of ethical business behaviour towards society and the environment. It means that sustainable consumption is prioritised and promoted by the company (FURNIEL, 2011).

To the extent that the population recognises that environmental problems not only impair the current quality of life, but also endanger the survival of humanity itself.

> Environmental education is the key to the successful implementation of any organisational system. No matter how well the system is structured, no matter how sophisticated the resources, the system will only work if people are sufficiently sensitised and trained to carry out their activities in an environmentally sound manner (MOREIRA, 2001, p.167).

Environmental education means learning to interact with the environment and realising that the results are very rewarding and change everything. It means having the conviction that you are doing something social and that you are responsible for the continuation of a healthy life for all of humanity.

> The environmental policy is the organisation's statement of its intentions and principles in relation to its overall environmental performance and provides a framework for action and the setting of its environmental objectives and targets. The environmental policy is therefore a statement of intent and can be seen as the compass of the system, as it sets out the guidelines it should follow and serves as the basis for setting and reviewing its objectives and targets (MOREIRA, 2001, p.92).

According to Alvarez (2010), there are several incentives for the introduction of environmental management methods:

- Internal stimuli:

- Need to reduce costs;
- Improved product quality;
- Improvement of the product and company image;
- The necessity of innovation;
- Greater social responsibility;
- Sensitisation of internal staff.

- External stimuli:

- The community;
- The market;
- The competition;
- The suppliers;
- The state.

2.2 The need for water reuse

Reusing water for irrigation is an alternative that is viable for several reasons: Water is generally scarce in the areas where crops need irrigation the most; irrigated agriculture requires large amounts of water, which is the largest water requirement in arid areas; crops can benefit not only from water but also, within certain limits, from substances dissolved in runoff such as humic substances, nitrogen, phosphorus, potassium and micronutrients (PESCOD, 1992).

Water reuse is a beneficial practice that can be observed in various ways. According to Van Der Hoeck et al. (2002), water reuse is beneficial when it enables the conservation of available water resources, contributes to the supply and recycling of nutrients, thereby reducing the use of chemical fertilisers, and when it is practicable for environmental conservation.

Although three quarters of our planet's surface is covered by water, it is important to remember that only a small proportion of freshwater can be utilised for most human activities without the need for major investment in adapting its physical, chemical and/or biological properties (Mays, 1996).

It should be noted that the availability of water in any location varies temporally and spatially due to the climatic conditions of each region and season and can be affected by human activities, whether due to excessive demand or pollution problems resulting from the discharge of domestic wastewater and industrial effluents.

Historically, water is a key element, as the colonisation of much of the world took place on the banks of watercourses, as in Brazil during the time of the Bandeirantes. With the increase in population and industrial growth, water was increasingly utilised as if it were an abundant and infinite resource. The concept of water abundance is even more pronounced today, especially in Brazil, one of the countries with the largest reserves of this resource: it has around 13 per cent of all the fresh water on earth (WRI, 2003).

However, a closer analysis reveals a different scenario. Water scarcity is not only a reality in areas with an unfavourable climate, but also in highly urbanised regions, such as metropolitan areas.

For this reason, it is important to develop strategies that enable sustainable water utilisation, as water resources are not abundant in the country. This means that the current concepts for water utilisation and the treatment and disposal of wastewater need to be reformulated. The rational utilisation and reuse of water has therefore become an essential element to ensure the continuity of human activities in this scenario of scarcity (MIERZWA; HESPANHOL, 2005).

The reuse of treated wastewater is an important resource for the implementation of sustainable water resource management, but we need to consider: more efficient water use and better management of systems, as well as the production of safe water for the desired purposes.

According to Giordano (n.d.), wastewater and the processes involved in its generation are conceptualised as follows:

> Water can be used by industry in a variety of ways: Admixture to the product; washing of machinery, pipes and floors; water from cooling systems and steam generators; water used directly in the industrial process stages or flowing into products; sanitary wastewater from employees. In general, some of this water is returned to nature as unusable waste, and when it reaches the rivers, it is heavily polluted and causes pollution.

The wastewater responsible for the environmental impact of industries that use water resources in their production chain is considered one of the main pollutants with long-lasting effects in the environment. Proof of this is the severity with which Brazilian legislation penalises companies that cause environmental disasters due to leaks and/or inadequate structures to preserve the health of the water used.

2.3 Legislation

Given the great importance of water for the development of various human activities, it was essential to create rules for the use of water resources by the various sectors of society, particularly for industry, wastewater disposal and rural products. Since its introduction, the main objective of the legislation has been to minimise pollution problems caused by the emission of wastewater into receiving waters.

The regulations are based on the concept of "command and control", i.e. federal and state authorities set quality standards for water resources and wastewater emissions that must be met by industry and other related activities. Compliance is then verified through inspections.

In Brazil, there is the National Environmental Council - CONAMA, which supplements and amends Resolution No. 357/2005 through Resolution No. 430 of 13 May 2011. It defines the conditions and standards for the discharge of wastewater. Taking into account the Federal Constitution of 1988 and Law No. 6.938 of 31 August 1981, which aim to control the discharge of pollutants into the environment and prohibit those that are considered harmful or dangerous to humans and other forms of life.

Article 2 of the Conama Resolution states that the discharge of waste water into the ground, even if treated, shall not be subject to the parameters and discharge standards laid down in this Resolution, but shall not cause pollution or contamination of surface water and groundwater.

Article 3 states that waste water from all sources of pollution may be discharged directly into receiving waters only after proper treatment and provided that it fulfils the conditions, standards and requirements laid down in this Resolution and other applicable regulations.

It is also worth considering the specifics, which are different in each region of the country, where states may have different rules as long as they are stricter than the federal resolution.

The entity responsible for the sources that potentially or actually pollute the water must submit to the competent environmental authority, by 31 March of each year, a declaration of pollution load for the previous calendar year, signed by the chief administrator of the company and the duly qualified technical manager, together with the corresponding certificate of technical responsibility (ART), as established in article 28 of CONAMA.

2.4 Industrial waste water

According to Sperling (1996), industrial wastewater exhibits great variability in its qualitative characteristics, making it difficult to generalise the most common values. With regard to the biological treatment of industrial wastewater, the following aspects and concepts are important:

- Biodegradability: the ability of wastewater to be stabilised by biochemical processes with microorganisms.

- Treatability: Possibility of treating the wastewater using conventional biological processes.
- Concentration of organic substances: Biochemical oxygen demand (BOD) of wastewater.
- Nutrient availability: Biological work requires a harmonious balance between the nutrients C:N:P (carbon, nitrogen, phosphorus).
- Toxicity: Certain industrial effluents contain toxic or inhibitory components that may impair or prevent biological treatment.

The characteristics of industrial wastewater vary largely depending on the type of industry and the industrial process used. In the case of the soft drinks industry, at least the following parameters should be analysed to characterise the wastewater: BOD or COD, suspended solids, oils and greases and pH.

The requirements for wastewater result from specific legislation that defines quality standards for the wastewater and the receiving waters. The removal of pollutants during treatment in order to fulfil these standards is associated with the terms treatment level and efficiency.

According to Sperling (1996), wastewater treatment is generally categorised into the following stages:

- **Preliminary:** only aims to remove coarse solids, sand. The basic removal mechanisms are of a physical nature, such as sieving and sedimentation. In addition, there is a flow measuring device, usually standardised flumes (Parshall flume), where the measured liquid level can be related to the flow rate, or rectangular or triangular overflow flumes. Coarse solids are usually removed using grids, rotary screens or crushers. The removal of coarse solids serves to protect the transport equipment (pumps, pipelines), the subsequent treatment and the collecting basins.

- **Primary clarification:** the aim is to remove the settleable solids and part of the organics (physical mechanism) by reducing them through simple processes such as sedimentation; this means a reduction in the BOD load, which is sent to secondary clarification, where their removal is somewhat more costly. Settling tanks can be circular or rectangular, with the effluent flowing slowly through the decanters, decanting the suspended solids with a lower density than the liquid, which rise to the surface of the decanters and are collected and removed for further treatment.

- **Secondary:** Biological mechanisms predominate here, the main aim of which is to remove organic matter and possibly nutrients (N and P). Organic matter exists in two forms: in dissolved form, which is not removed by purely physical processes during primary treatment, and as suspended solids, most of which is removed during primary treatment, but the more slowly degradable solids remain in the liquid mass. The secondary treatment processes are intended to accelerate the degradation processes that occur naturally in the receiving waters and achieve the degradation of degradable organic pollutants under controlled conditions in shorter time intervals than in natural systems. This process involves a variety of microorganisms (bacteria, protozoa, fungi, etc.) that come into contact with the organic material in the wastewater, utilise it as food and convert the organic material into carbon dioxide, water and cellular material. This decomposition requires the presence of oxygen as a basic component of aerobic processes, as well as other favourable conditions such as temperature, pH, contact time, etc. Secondary treatment generally includes pre-treatment equipment, but may also include primary treatment equipment. There are a variety of secondary treatment processes, the most common of which are Stabilisation ponds and variants, activated sludge and variants, biological filters and variants, anaerobic treatment, landfill (a mixture of treatment and final disposal classified as secondary treatment due to the action of biological mechanisms and their high efficiency in pollutant removal).

- **Tertiary treatment:** aims to remove certain pollutants, usually toxic or non-biodegradable compounds, or to complement the removal of pollutants that are not sufficiently removed during secondary treatment. This treatment is very rare in Brazil.

2.5 Fertigation

Industrial development is one of the main causes of water pollution, whether through negligence in the treatment of waste before it is discharged into watercourses or through increasingly frequent accidents and carelessness that lead to the release of numerous pollutants into watercourses, thus harming the environment. In the face of increasingly stringent environmental regulations, it is important to strive for continuous improvement with cleaner technologies that help prevent the waste of natural resources and ensure adequate waste treatment, significantly reducing the environmental and financial impact of fines for environmental offences (RATTI E PASSIG, 2007).

The use of industrial wastewater has become a complementary source of water and nutrients for irrigation, as well as the investigation of alternatives to the use of nutrients from wastewater, which is not new. According to Braile (1979), the application of vinasse or restilo to the soil as a method of irrigating crops was first carried out in Brazil in the state of Pernambuco.

Fertilisation is very efficient as it combines two main factors that are important for the growth and development of plants: Water and nutrients. Threadgill (1985) states that in the USA about 4.3 million hectares are cultivated in this way at least once a year. The annual increase in fertigation in this country is about 8 to 9 %, which shows its importance for irrigated crops.

Although fertilisation has advantages, there is a lack of information on the subject. According to COSTA et al. (1986), although fertigation is applied in some irrigated areas of Brazil, the lack of information, especially on the dosage, the type of fertiliser most recommended, the prevention of precipitate formation and the method and timing of application, shows that it is necessary to carry out research in this area that takes into account the different conditions of the country.

Prieto (1985) states that, in theory, any irrigation method can be used for the supply and application of chemical products together with water, but that the uniform distribution of methods that carry water in closed, pressurised pipes is better suited to this practice. Depending on the irrigation system and the care taken when carrying out fertigation, various advantages can be achieved compared to conventional fertilisation methods, such as

- Better utilisation of the irrigation systems, which leads to higher profitability and better use of the invested capital;
- Application of nutrients at the exact time and in the exact quantity required by the plants;

- Less labour required for fertilisation, as practically the same labour is used as for irrigation; less compaction due to less machine traffic on the land, as is the case with traditional fertilisation methods; less physical damage to crops for the same reasons as mentioned in the previous point, as the cutting of flowers, fruits and plant branches is avoided, which reduces the occurrence and spread of pests and diseases;
- Application of micronutrients: When fertilising in small doses per area, it is generally difficult to achieve good uniformity of fertiliser distribution using manual methods, which is easily possible with fertigation;
- Can be used in various irrigation systems;
- increased productivity and commercial product quality;
- good uniformity of fertiliser distribution in the soil if there is also good uniformity of water distribution through the irrigation system.
- Some falsifications that can occur are due to failure to consider technical aspects related to plant nutrition, soil chemistry and physics, plant

physiology, water, climate and irrigation practices themselves. Limitations include:

- the need for technical knowledge of fertilisers and dosage calculations;
- the need for trained personnel to handle the fertilisers and injectors;
- Environmental damage caused by the pollution of water sources;
- the possibility of corrosion problems in irrigation systems;
- Demand for toxicity problems for farmers and problems with toxicity and burning of plant leaves;
- Increase in the initial cost of the irrigation system;
- increased pressure losses in the irrigation system.

In order to achieve appropriate fertilisation, certain factors must be taken into account and correctly analysed. These factors may be of greater or lesser importance depending on the intended use. The factors are:

- the different types of fertilisers used in fertilisation;
- Factors related to plant nutrition;
- on the type of soil;
- the quality of the irrigation water;
- Plant species;
- the type of injector used in the irrigation system;
- the cost-benefit ratio;
- Product corrosion;
- Pollution of the environment;
- other factors (compatibility between the products; position of the injector in the system; concentration, injection rate; rates; application time; quantity and uniformity of application of the products in the irrigation water).

It should be borne in mind that the success of fertilisation depends on good irrigation planning and execution. Excessive irrigation can increase nutrient losses, especially nitrogen, which can contaminate underground and surface aquifers.

Irrigation has proven to be more efficient in providing nutrients to different crops and has a number of advantages over the traditional method (Alvarenga, 1999). This technique, using the same irrigation system, makes it possible to dose and divide the fertilisers in the desired way, saving labour, reducing leaching and distributing nutrients better in the soil profile (Wiersma, 1969; Pompa, 1974). According to Raposo (1979), it facilitates top dressing in dense crops and doses the nutrient quantities precisely according to the absorption behaviour of the plants.

2.6 Water quality parameters

According to Sperling (1996), water quality can be represented by different parameters reflecting the main physical, chemical and biological properties, as we will see in the following points, which are generally used to characterise water supplies, effluents, springs and receiving waters:

Physical water quality parameters

a) Colour: The colour of water is the result of the dissolved substances. In its pure state and in large quantities, water is bluish in colour. If it is rich in iron, it is purple in colour. If it is rich in manganese, it is black and if it is rich in humic acids, it is yellowish in colour. The colour of the water is measured by comparison with known platinum-cobalt solutions or with glass discs calibrated with the platinum-cobalt solution. The operating permit states: It must not change the colour (true colour) of the receiving body.

b) **Turbidity**: It is the measure of how a ray of light passes through a certain amount of water. Turbidity is caused by solids in suspension (sludge, clay, colloids, organic matter, etc.). Turbidity is measured with a turbidimeter by comparing the scattering of a light beam as it passes through the sample with the scattering of a beam of the same intensity as it passes through a standard suspension. The stronger the scattering, the higher the turbidity. The values are given in nephelometric turbidity units (UNT).

c) **Odour and** taste: Odour and taste are two sensory impressions that manifest themselves together and are therefore difficult to separate. The odour and taste of water depends on the dissolved salts and gases. As the human palate reacts with varying degrees of sensitivity to different salts, a few milligrams per litre of some salts (e.g. iron and copper) are perceptible, while several hundred milligrams of sodium chloride are not. According to the operating licence: Free from unpleasant odours.

d) **Temperature:** Groundwater has a small temperature range, i.e. its temperature is not affected by changes in atmospheric temperature. The aquifers near the surface are an exception. At greater depths, the water temperature is influenced by the local geothermal degree. According to the operating licence: <40°C.

Chemical parameters of the water quality

a) **Ph:** When water molecules ionise, they split into H+ and OH+ ions. The pH value is defined as the decimal logarithm of the effective concentration or activity of the ions in the water that cause the pH value to be greater than 7.0 (more hydroxyl groups) or less (more H+ cations). According to the operating licence: pH value between 6.0 and 9.0.
From an analytical point of view, the pH value is one of the most important parameters for the determination of most chemical species of interest in both drinking water and wastewater analysis.

b) **Alkalinity:** Chemically speaking, alkalinity is the inverse property of acidity, i.e. the ability to neutralise acids. In general, the presence of alkalinity brings the pH value above 7.0, but a lower pH value (above 4) does not mean that no alkaline substances are dissolved in the aqueous medium.

c) **Acidity:** Acidity is the ability to neutralise alkaline solutions, i.e. the ability of water to resist pH changes caused by the introduction of bases. In general, acidity is associated with the presence of free CO_2. The presence of organic acids is more common in surface waters than in groundwater.

d) **Hardness:** This parameter characterises the quality of industrial and household water. Relatively high maximum values are permitted for drinking water, which are typical of hard or very hard water. Almost all water hardness is caused by the presence of calcium and magnesium salts (bicarbonates, sulphates, chlorides and nitrates) in solution.

e) **Iron:** It is found in many types of soil and is one of the most abundant chemical elements in natural waters. The iron contained in the water can come from the sources themselves and from the collection or supply systems through the corrosion of metal surfaces or even from industrial waste.

f) **Chlorides:** The presence of chlorides in water results from the dissolution of salts with CL ions, for example sodium chloride. It is characteristic of seawater, the content of which is close to 20000 ppm, with sodium chloride (Na Cl) being the most present at around 70 % of this content.

g) **Nitrogen:** Nitrogen occurs in various forms and oxidation states in the aquatic environment: molecular (N_2), organic, ammonia (NH_4), nitrite (NO_2) and nitrate (NO_3). As an essential element for the development of algae, high concentrations of nitrogen, especially in stagnant or laminar waters, can lead to excessive growth of these organisms, which is known as eutrophication. According to the operating licence: <= 20 mg NTK/L or 75% efficiency.

h) **Phosphorus:** Like nitrogen, phosphorus is an essential nutrient for the growth of microorganisms responsible for the biodegradation of organic matter, as well as for the growth of algae, which can promote the occurrence of eutrophication in water sources. The nutrient in the waters usually comes from household and certain industrial waste, but can also come from the dissolution of soil compounds. According to the operating licence: <= 3 mg P/L or 75 % efficiency.

i) **Dissolved oxygen (DO):** is essential for aerobic organisms (which live in the presence of oxygen). During the stabilisation of organic matter, bacteria consume oxygen in their respiration processes, which can lead to a reduction in its concentration in the environment. Depending on the extent of this phenomenon, various aquatic organisms may die.

j) **Inorganic micropollutants:** A large proportion of inorganic micropollutants are toxic, especially heavy metals (arsenic,

cadmium, chromium, lead, mercury and silver). In addition to heavy metals, there are other inorganic micropollutants such as cyanides, fluoride and others that are important for public health. They originate less from natural sources, but are due to human influence: Industrial waste, mining and quarrying, agriculture. Heavy metals are toxic to aquatic life and water users.

k) **Organic micropollutants:** Some organic substances are resistant to biodegradation and accumulate at a certain point in the cycle. These include pesticides, some types of cleaning agents and a large number of chemical products. A large proportion of these compounds are associated with toxicity problems even in low concentrations. They originate naturally from woody plants (tannin, lignin, cellulose, phenols). And through human influence: Industrial waste, detergents, oil processing and refining, pesticides.

l) **Organic matter:** The organic matter present in water bodies and wastewater is a feature of major importance that causes the main problem of water pollution: the consumption of dissolved oxygen by microorganisms in their processes of utilisation and stabilisation of organic matter.

The most important organic components are protein compounds, carbohydrates, fats and oils as well as urea, surfactants, phenols, pesticides and others in smaller quantities. It is very difficult to determine the various components of organic matter in wastewater in the laboratory, as they can take on different forms and compounds.

Indirect methods are therefore used to characterise organic substances or their pollution potential: Measurement of oxygen consumption (COD and BOD) and measurement of organic carbon (TOC). BOD is traditionally the most widely used parameter to characterise the pollution level of a water body and is used to characterise raw and treated wastewater.

It is produced naturally: by organic plant and animal matter and by human influence (household and industrial waste).

j) **Biochemical oxygen demand (BOD):** This is the most widely used method for measuring the amount of organic matter present. The amount of organic matter is important for determining the degree of pollution of a wastewater, dimensioning wastewater treatment plants and measuring their efficiency. [2]According to the operating licence: <= 80mg O /L.

k) **Chemical oxygen demand (COD):** The COD test corresponds to the amount of oxygen in a sample that can be oxidised by permanganate or potassium dichromate in an acidic solution. It is used to measure organic substances in wastewater, industrial and municipal water that contain compounds toxic to biological life. [2]According to the operating licence: <= 300mg O /L.

The COD is always higher than the BOD, as more compounds can be oxidised chemically than biologically.

Microorganisms perform various functions of fundamental importance, especially those related to the transformation of substances. Another important aspect of the biological quality of water is the possibility of disease transmission, as water can indirectly transmit diseases through organisms of the coliform group.

The following issues should be considered when reusing water: the presence of pathogenic organisms, contamination of aquifers, heavy metals, physical degradation of the soil and the increase of sodium (Na) concentration in the soil. Water reuse systems should be subject to criteria and quality standards that take into account and emphasise public health, water acceptability, environmental protection, the quality of the water source for reuse and the suitability of the quality for the intended use (MANANCUSO et. All, 2003).

According to Sperling (1996), microorganisms in wastewater can be classified as plants or animals. The most important microscopic plants are bacteria, fungi and algae. Microscopic animals include protozoa, rotifers, crustaceans and nematodes. Typical species are listed below:

a) **Bacteria** - They are categorised as plants because they only feed on soluble food. Insoluble organic elements must be hydrolysed or dissolved in the cell walls before metabolism. Carbohydrates and proteins can be easily hydrolysed to produce soluble substances that can then diffuse into the bacteria. Long-chain fatty acids, alcohols and hydrocarbons tend to dissolve on the cell surface.

b) **Fungi** - They are multicellular and, like unicellular bacteria, can feed on all types of soluble organic substances. Unlike bacteria, however, they are strictly aerobic. Fungi therefore need dissolved oxygen to survive and grow.

c) **Algae** - These are unicellular and multicellular photosynthetic plants that extract enough energy from sunlight to produce new cells. Although inorganic compounds are the main food source, some species can feed on organic compounds in the absence of light. Oxygen is an important by-product of algal metabolism.

d) **Protozoa** - These are single-celled animals that can be easily observed under a microscope at 100x magnification. Bacteria and algae are the primary food source for advanced forms of protozoa. The four basic groups of protozoa that are important to the chemistry of drinking water are: sacardina, mastigophora, ciliata, suctoria.

e) **Viruses** - These are parasitic organisms that are created by the combination of genetic material (DNA or RNA) and a protein envelope. They cause diseases and can be difficult to remove during water or wastewater treatment.

f) **Helminths** - These are higher animals. Helminth eggs present in wastewater can cause diseases.

Chapter 3 DESCRIPTION OF THE OPERATION OF THE AIR CONDITIONING SYSTEM

The wastewater treatment plant is used to treat all wastewater produced during the company's production processes, as well as wastewater from the canteen and toilets.

All liquid industrial waste is generated during beverage production and includes the following types:

- Wash bottles;
- Leftover soft drinks from the supermarket;
- Wash the equipment to disinfect it;
- Cleaning the floors;
- Discharge of the boiler;
- Discharge from cooling towers;
- Discharge of flocculation and other wastewater from the wastewater treatment plant;
- Dumping of non-compliant products;
- Cleaning the activated charcoal filter;

3.1 Primary treatment

All wastewater from the factory, including sanitary wastewater, first enters tank 1, where it is first separated from the liquid by the solids, and is then channelled into the Parshall channel, which is used to measure the liquid flow.

3.2 Oil and water separator box

The decanted water is sent for primary treatment and the oil is collected and stored in the restricted area for hazardous waste. This collection is carried out by an employee if necessary.

3.3 Equalising basin

The equalisation tank makes it possible to compensate for fluctuations in the flow and composition of the waste water from the primary treatment without affecting the process. The tank is agitated by a pump that must be activated to prevent odour nuisance that could affect the air quality. Next to the pump for agitating the equalisation tank is a device for measuring the redox potential, which is used to detect oxygen reducers that could affect the system.

3.4 Conditioning tank

Its purpose is to adjust the pH value of the wastewater for subsequent decomposition by the anaerobic bacteria. This adjustment is controlled by the pH meter upstream of the reactor.

3.5 Anaerobic reactor with internal circuit

Their purpose is the decomposition of organic substances by anaerobic microorganisms. During this decomposition, a large proportion of the substances are converted into biogas (carbon dioxide and methane). The resulting biogas is channelled into the fireplace and burned there.

The treated wastewater from the reactor circulates continuously with the treatment tank and is automatically channelled into the aeration lagoon when a certain volume is reached.

3.6 Aerated lagoon with complete mixing

It is used to break down the organic substances from the reactor wastewater through aeration, which supplies oxygen to the microorganisms and prevents the settling of bacterial flocs.

3.7 Settling pond

It is used to sediment the sludge remaining in the wastewater and feed the sludge into the compressor and the water into the process.

3.8 Panfloc

It serves to contain the impurities contained in the wastewater.

3.9 Contact Tank

It is used to add chlorine to the wastewater.

3.10 Zeolite filter

It is activated by chlorine and has the task of reducing the concentration of iron and aluminium in wastewater.

3.11 Carbon filter

The carbon filter has the task of reducing the colour of the waste water and retaining the chlorine.

3.12 Presser

The compressor has the task of removing the sludge present in the wastewater by feeding the sludge into the drying bed and the wastewater into the treatment plant.

As soon as the wastewater has passed through this process, it is considered treated wastewater, i.e. all wastewater that fulfils the required parameters. However, internal checks with laboratory analyses and external analyses prescribed by the environmental authorities are carried out for this purpose.

Therefore, the characteristics of this wastewater that limit its application to the soil are determined by the balances of water, nutrients such as nitrogen and phosphorus, organic matter and other constituents present in significant concentrations. In general, the application system is controlled by the hydraulic application rate or application rate, i.e. the volume of water applied per unit area in a given period REZENDE (2003).

The parameters for determining the application rate depend on the water requirements of the plants, the soil and water characteristics, the type of plants, the risk of salinisation and contamination of the soil or the ability of the soil and plants to assimilate the applied waste. If a plant is grown in the disposal area, it must be tolerant to the excess water and the components of the wastewater (FEIGIN et al., 1991).

The main advantages of using this treated wastewater are that it conserves available water, it is widely available, it allows nutrients to be added and reused (reducing the need for chemical fertilisers) and it helps to protect the environment (van der HOEK et al., 2002).

When wastewater is applied to the soil surface in a controlled manner, it can undergo a higher degree of treatment through physical, chemical and biological processes in the soil-water-plant system. The soil, as a living and dynamic system characterised by its large active surface area and the result of physical, chemical and biological processes, reacts strongly with the components of the applied wastewater. ^{22}The organic compounds decompose into CO , H O and other inorganic compounds. The inorganic components can be exchanged, adsorbed or precipitated by chemical reactions that convert them into poorly soluble compounds, or they can be adsorbed by the plants and thus partially removed from the soil solution: In this way, the soil and plants act as real "living filters", absorbing and retaining pollutants and pathogenic organisms in waste and wastewater (FEIGIN et al., 1991).

Plants grow and develop by absorbing water and mineral elements from the soil and carbon dioxide (CO_2) through their leaves. A number of mineral elements are required individually, as growth and development can only take place if they are all present in sufficient quantities.

Nitrogen (N) - is considered the element of quality, as it is part of the protein composition of all plants and animals and is essential for the formation of organic compounds. It acts in all phases of the plant: growth, flowering and fruit formation.

Phosphorus (P) - no other element can replace it, plants cannot live without it! It is a component of the energy conversion process, photosynthesis, sugar metabolism, energy storage and transfer, cell division, cell enlargement and the transfer of genetic information. It promotes initial formation, root development and plant growth.

Potassium (K) - interacts with almost all essential plant nutrients. Unlike other nutrients, this element does not form compounds in plants, but remains free to "regulate" many important processes. Its most important functions are: Enzyme activation, photosynthesis, efficient water utilisation, starch formation and protein synthesis.

Calcium (Ca) - this element contributes to fertility and to plants that are intensively cultivated or under stress. It promotes the strengthening of all plant organs, especially roots and leaves. It is a component of the plant cell wall and is necessary for maintaining its structure and activating amylase. It is also important for maintaining the balance between alkalinity and acidity in the environment and in plant sap.

Magnesium (Mg) - this element is an essential component of chlorophyll, the pigment responsible for photosynthesis and the green colour of plants.

Sulphur (S) - along with N, P and K, an important nutrient for plant development. It is required for the formation of amino acids and proteins as well as for cold resistance. Legumes need the element for nodule formation and nitrogen fixation from the air and forage plants for production.

Boron (B) - is important for cell growth, especially in the younger parts of the plant. It is required for the formation of proteins and plays a role in pollination, seed development, cell wall formation, flowering and flower set, the formation of legume nodules, the growth of branches and fruits.

Copper (Cu) - as a component of metalloenzymes and as an intermediate electron receptor, it plays an important role in photosynthesis, respiration, reduction and nitrogen fixation.

^{2}**Chlorine (Cl)** - is involved in photosynthesis, in particular in the splitting of the water molecule (H O) in the presence of light. This element activates various enzymes and is involved in the transport of cations within the plant.

Iron (Fe) - acts as a catalyser in the formation of chlorophyll and as an oxygen carrier. It is essential for protein synthesis and the formation of some enzymatic respiratory systems.

Manganese (Mn) - is an enzyme activator that controls the oxidation-reduction reactions important for photosynthesis and chlorophyll synthesis.

Molybdenum (Mo) - is necessary for the synthesis and activation of nitrate reductase in the plant. It is also required for the symbiotic fixation of nitrogen by the bacteria living in the root nodules of legumes.

Zinc (Zn) - is an enzyme activator in plants. It controls the production of important growth regulators that influence new growth and development.

Chapter 4 METHODOLOGY

According to the definition of the objectives to be achieved with this study, the research conducted aims to determine the feasibility of fertigation as a method to reuse water in the factory through exploratory research, as there has been no previous research on this project.

The aim of this work is to evaluate the chemical parameters of the treated wastewater in order to determine whether it can be used for fertilisation. For this purpose, the technical reports on the wastewater from the wastewater treatment plant from 2012 and 2013 listed below are used. This evaluation is possible because the company monitors the parameters through monthly analyses in order to respond to the environmental authorities. By evaluating these analyses, we can quantify the nutrients contained in these effluents and apply them to the soil in an appropriate manner, taking into account saturation capacity, infiltration and compliance with environmental principles.

PARAMETERS	JANUARY	FEBRUARY	MARCH	APRIL	MAY	JUNE	JULY	AUGUST	SEPTEMBER	OCTOBER	NOVEMBER	DECEMBER	LO STANDARD
COD		9,8	38	24	58	32	32	9	13	30	2,35	33	<= 300 mg/l
BSB		7,8	13	5,8	18	8	16	15			27	13	<= 80 mg/l
TOTAL PHOSPHOR	2,42	2,82	2,75	2,6	4,96	4,66	1,68	3,36	15,9	0,89	2,4	3,44	<= 3 mg/l
NITROGEN		6,8	4,06	2,64	2,85				38,1		1,31		<= 20 mg/l
SOLID DEPOSITS	7,5	20	0,3	<0,1	<0,1	<0,1	<0,1	<0,1	<0,1	<0,1	<0,1	<0,1	<= 1.0 mg/l
COLIFORMES	<0,1	<100	310	<100	<100	<100	<100	<100	<100	<100	<100	300	<= 100000 MPN/100ml
PH		7,6	7,5	7,69	7,62	7,72	7,64	7	4,7		7,81	7,86	between 6.0 and 9.0

Table 1: Report for 2012

PARAMETERS	JANUARY	FEBRUARY	MARCH	APRIL	MAY	JUNE	JULY	AUGUST	SEPTEMBER	OCTOBER	NOVEMBER	DECEMBER	LO STANDARD
COD		9,88	19	24	49	43	32	9	38	28	6,39	5,91	<= 300 mg/l
BSB	15	3,3		8	16	14	12	27	13	12	9,72	14,7	<= 80 mg/l
TOTAL PHOSPHOR	2,42	1,84		2,64	1,86	2,56	0,7	2,2	1,36	0,89	2,35	2,14	<= 3 mg/l
NITROGEN		6,37	3,68	3,34	2,35	0,42	2,91	1,48					<= 20 mg/l
SOLID DEPOSITS	<0,1	<0,1	<0,1	<0,1	<0,1	<0,1	<0,1	<0,1	<0,2	<0,1	<0,1	<0,1	<= 1.0 mg/l
COLIFORMES	1007,5	200		410	310	520	<100	200	310	<100	<100	<100	<= 100000 MPN/100ml
PH		7,88	7,78	7,81	7,81	7,92	7,76			7,73	7,81	7,75	between 6.0 and 9.0

Table 2: Report for 2013

These technical reports are drawn up by the ALAC laboratory, which provides the company with outsourced services corresponding to the analyses of the parameters required by the installation's operating licence.

PARAMETERS	UNIT	METHOD	
COD	mg/l	Standard methods 22st-Method 5220 B [PNT013-EF]	Closed-loop reflux spectrophotometry
BSB	mg/l	Standard methods 22st-Method 5210 B [PNT017-EF]	Dilution and incubation method (20°C, 5 days)
TOTAL PHOSPHOR	mg/l	Standard methods 22st-Method 4500- S/W and E [PNT021-EF]	Colourimetric method
NITROGEN	mg/l	Standard methods 22st-Method 4500 Norg-B and D/4500 NH3-C [PNT024-EF]	Titrimetric method
DEDUCTIBLE SUBSTANCES	mg/l	Standard methods 22st-Method 2540 F [PNT005-EF]	Imhoff cone method
COLIFORMES	MPN/ml	Standard methods 22st-Method 9223 [PNT006-EF]	Determination of the Most Probable Number of Escherichia coli by enzymatic substrate.

Table 3: Method used by the ALAC laboratory.

Chapter 5 RESULTS AND DISCUSSIONS

Based on these reports, we can see that the results for the parameters are within the legal limits, which allows us to check the feasibility of using this wastewater for fertilisation.

Phosphorus is one of the essential nutrients for the plant, it acts in respiration and energy production, in the reports we found that in 2012 it appeared altered in the months of May, June, August and December and remained stable in 2013, in terms of fertilisation we will not have a problem as we have control over the amount present and the amount necessary for the growth and proper development of the plant.Nitrogen is essential for the plant in the formation of proteins, that is, substances that are part of the plant tissue. In 2012, a change was detected in the reports submitted and, as the quantities were far below the norm, the nitrogen was not analysed for several months.We also found that the thermotolerant coliforms were below the limit, although it is recommended for the fertilisation process to chlorinate the wastewater to ensure the effectiveness of the system without causing microbiological contamination, considering the proximity of the water table, because we must be careful not to contaminate but to enrich by providing the nutrients essential for plant development.If we compare the analysis reports for 2012 and 2013, we see that in 2012 two parameters were exceptionally above the norms and that in 2013 all parameters stabilised. This justifies the fact that the monthly monitoring of all these parameters has improved every year, which has led to an improvement in the analysis results, so that in 2013 none of the parameters are outside the norm.we lean on the fact that every year the Vonpar company sets itself objectives to reduce water consumption by avoiding waste and promoting the reuse of water in order to preserve the water resources in its territory.In this sense of preserving water resources, this study aims to form an ecologically correct water cycle, in which the wastewater produced is treated and then incorporated into the soil in an appropriate manner to ensure the sustainable development of the ecosystem. Taking into account the results of the analysis and verification of the availability of the land for application and the limits of nutrient uptake by the plants, a study was carried out to monitor the runoff of these effluents, as shown in the table below. below.

DAY	TIME	FLOW	REMARKS
01/10/2013	09:00	131	
02/10/2013	09:00	128	
03/10/2013	09:00	106	
04/10/2013	09:00	80	
05/10/2013	09:00	82	
06/10/2013	09:00		Shutdown at the factory
07/10/2013	09:00	129	
08/10/2013	09:00	130	
09/10/2013	09:00	117	
10/10/2013	09:00	100	
11/10/2013	09:00		Shutdown at the factory
12/10/2013	09:00		Shutdown at the factory
13/10/2013	09:00	128	
14/10/2013	09:00	121	
15/10/2013	09:00	116	
16/10/2013	09:00	87	
17/10/2013	09:00	86	
18/10/2013	09:00	76	
19/10/2013	09:00	80	Shutdown at the factory
20/10/2013	09:00		Shutdown at the factory
21/10/2013	09:00	132	
22/10/2013	09:00	123	
23/10/2013	09:00	125	
24/10/2013	09:00	125	
25/10/2013	09:00	115	
26/10/2013	09:00		Shutdown at the factory
27/10/2013	09:00		Shutdown at the factory
28/10/2013	09:00	124	
29/10/2013	09:00	114	
30/10/2013	09:00	130	
31/10/2013	10:00	110	

Table 4: ei flow fluent in 20 13

This table shows that the average wastewater flow rate was 111 m/h, with the treatment plant operating 16 hours a day from Monday to Saturday.

The work is being carried out at Gama's wastewater treatment plant and is focussed on three areas.

Figure 1: Area 1 with an area of around 1800 m2

Figure 2: Area 2 with a length of approx. 2400 m^2

Figure 3: Area 3 with an area of around 1800 m2

Lawns are laid throughout the company's premises, which has many environmental benefits. [22]A well-maintained lawn provides a comfortable and safe place for fun and sport; it releases oxygen (about 230 metres of lawn release enough O for four people); it cools the air, contributing to efforts to reduce the global warming trend (on a hot summer's day, a lawn has a temperature 16.5°C and 7.8°C lower than tarmac and bare ground respectively); reduces CO emissions (they absorb a large amount of CO 7.8°C lower than tarmac and bare soil respectively); reduces CO emissions (they absorb a large amount of CO to photosynthesise throughout the year), mitigating the greenhouse effect; and controls soil pollution (the rhizosphere acts as a filter, absorbing everything that passes through it). Another positive effect of turf on the environment is the control of soil erosion. Turf is six times more effective at absorbing rainwater than wheat and four times more effective than hay (Beard, 1985).

However, in order for lawns to fulfil all these benefits, they must be adequately supplied with all the important minerals so that they can grow well and maintain their quality. As most soils do not have enough nutrients to meet the lawn's needs, it is necessary to supply them through fertilisation.

On average, we had 3mg/l of phosphorus and 6mg/l of nitrogen in 2012 and 2013. If you look at the average flow for these years of 111m/day and convert the flow in litres to 111,000l/day, you get a total of 333,000mg P and 666,000 N. If this wastewater is applied to an area of 6,000 metres at this flow rate, the result is an application of 55 mg/m phosphorus and 111 mg/m nitrogen.

Considering that the wastewater treatment plant operates for 16 hours a day over an area of 6,000 m2 , 55 mg of phosphorus and 111 mg of nitrogen are available per 1 metre of surface area, and this data is monitored to control and check the saturation of these nutrients in the plant and the infiltration of the wastewater into the soil.

Furthermore, considering that grass plants require 300 mg/ha of nitrogen per day, so that for 10,000 m 300 mg of nitrogen are required, and considering that the area available for the application of this project is 6.[22] Considering that the availability of nitrogen from this effluent is lower than the needs of the plants, this facilitates the control of the application of this nutrient and by visually monitoring the grass by colouring, we can check the saturation or lack of nitrogen and phosphorus that may occur in the plant.

This test shows that the amount of nitrogen available is greater than the amount of phosphorus, which favours cultivation, as nitrogen is the most important nutrient for feeding grasses and is needed in much greater quantities than any other nutrient. Nitrogen can be lost through leaching (water seeps through the soil profile and takes the nitrogen with it) or in the form of gases (through denitrification or volatilisation), be unavailable to plants for a period of time as it is consumed in the structure of soil microorganisms (immobilisation), or be released into the soil through the mineralisation of organic matter.

Knowing the two main effects of nitrogen on the nutrition of grasses makes it easier to understand the two main symptoms of nitrogen deficiency in lawns. The first is a reduction in the growth of the vegetative part, especially the leaves. A reduction in growth due to nitrogen deficiency can be recognised, for example, by a decrease in the amount of clippings collected after mowing a particular area. The second symptom of nitrogen deficiency is the yellowing of the leaves due to a reduction in chlorophyll concentration. In addition to these two main symptoms of nitrogen deficiency, lawns may exhibit excessive flowering when there is a lack of available nitrogen (Christians, 1998).

An excess of nitrogen can lead to excessive growth of the above-ground part (the leaves) and a reduction in root growth. Another problem with an excess of nitrogen is that it makes the grass more susceptible to attack by pathogens.

(disease-causing microorganisms) and pests due to the increased growth of the leaves, which have a thinner cuticle layer.

Another nutrient observed is phosphorus, which is essential for root growth, and grasses grown on phosphorus-deficient soils are unable to develop a well-developed root system (Christians, 1998).

Phosphorus is not very mobile in our soils as it is bound in Fe and Al oxides and is therefore not available to the plant. In order for the phosphorus to be absorbed efficiently, the fertiliser must be applied as close to the roots as possible and in a higher dose to compensate for the phosphorus bound by the oxides so that there is enough left for the grass.

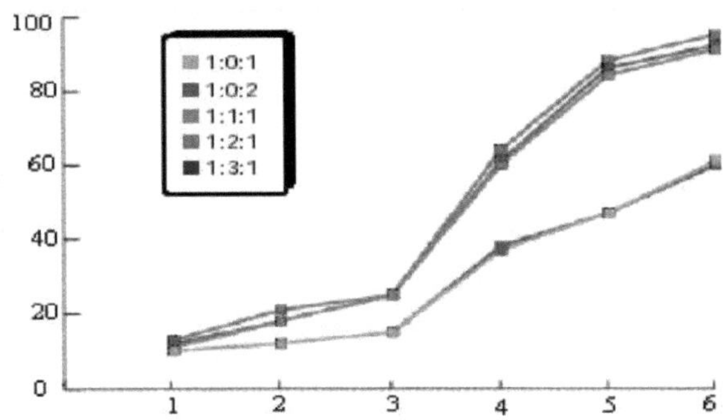

Figure 4 - Percentage soil cover by TifEagle bermudagrass depending on the NPK ratio of the fertiliser up to six weeks after planting the runners.
(Adapted from Rodriguez et al., 2000).

In established lawns, the root system is already well developed and occupies a large part of the soil under the vegetative part of the lawn to a depth of 10 to 15 cm. This allows the lawn to make efficient use of the available phosphorus in the soil and the fertiliser, as the fertiliser is close to the roots wherever it is applied and is absorbed by them.

In addition to a less developed root system, one of the symptoms of phosphorus deficiency is a dark green colouration of the older leaves, which turn purple at the edges (Turner, 1993). However, this symptom is very rare in lawns and can be confused with the effects of low temperatures and light in winter on some summer grasses.

This work shows that fertilisation with industrial effluents is feasible, as these effluents contain many nutrients that significantly support the growth process of the plants, make them more resistant, bring economic benefits and improve the quality of the grass, which leads to the conclusion that it is feasible as long as proper management is introduced in the implementation of this project.

Chapter 6 CONCLUSION

With regard to the reuse of water, this work investigated the utilisation of waste water behind the irrigation system on an available area of the company, which consists mainly of grasses.

The technical reports on this wastewater have confirmed that it can be incorporated into agricultural soils so that it can return to the water cycle of this environment.

[22]This study found that the nitrogen and phosphorus concentrations of this wastewater were below the daily limits for these two nutrients at 111 mg/m and 55 mg/m respectively, and that grass plants require 300 mg per day of each nutrient.

[32]Considering the concentration of this wastewater compared to the amount required for the growth of the grasses, it can be concluded that with a daily flow of 111 m/day in an area of 6000 m, a modest irrigation system is quite feasible, requiring only monitoring.

REFERENCES

ALVAREZ, Maria Esmeralda Ballestero. **Quality, production and farm management.** São Paulo:_ Atlas, 2010.

BEARD, J.B. An assessment of turfgrass water use. *Turfgrass Water Conservation.* Univ. of California Division of Agriculture & Natural Resources, 1985. http://www.turgrasssod.org/trc/statistics.html. Retrieved on: 02/11/2014.

BRAILE, P.M. **Manual de tratamento de aguas residuárias industriais**. São Paulo Cetesb, 1979.

CHRISTIANS, N.E. *Fundamentals of turfgrass management,* Arbor Press, Chelsea, MI, 1998, 301p.

COSTA, E.F.; FRANÇA, G.E; ALVES, V.M.C. Fertiliser application via irrigation water. **III Course on the utilisation and management of irrigation**. Informe Agropecuário. Belo Horizonte, 1986.

DONAIRE, Denis. **Environmental management in the company**. Editora Atlas S.A. 2 Ed. São Paulo:1999.

DIAS, Reinaldo. **Environmental Management: Social Responsibility and Sustainability**. São Paulo: Atas, 2006.

GIL, Antônio Carlos. **Methods and techniques of social research.** 5th edition. São Paulo: Atlas, 1999.

GANDHI, Giordano. **Treatment and control of industrial wastewater**. Available at <ww2.uerj.br/~ambiente/destaque/proj pesq meio amb.pdf> . accessed on 12 June 2014.

MIERZWA, J. C.; HESPANHOL, I. **Águas na indústria: uso racional e reuso**. São Paulo: Oficina de Textos, 2005.

MAYS, L.W.**Walter Resources: an introduction. In: Handbook of Water Resources**. New York: McGraw-Hill, 1996.

MORAN, J. M.;MORGAN, D. M.;WIERSMA,J.H. **Introduction to Environmental Science**. 2nd edition. New York: W.H. Freeman and Company, 1985.

MANCUSO, P.C.S.; SANTOS, H.F. **Water reuse**. University of São Paulo. School of Public Health. Information Centre for Environment and Health, SP; Monole, 2003, 579 p. (Collection Environment).

MIRANDA, Mazarelo Carneiro. **KEEPING AN EYE ON THE ENVIRONMENT**. Available at:< http://www.techoje.com.br/site/techoje/categoria/detalhe article/132>. Retrieved on: 03 June 2014.

WHAT IS ISO 14001 - a step-by-step guide to applying an environmental system. Available at: < http://www.bsibrasil.com.br/documentos/What is 14KBR.pdf>. Retrieved on: 10 June 2014.

WHAT IS THE ISO 14001 STANDARD? Available at:< http://www.evsbrasil.com.br/CertificacaoISO14001.htm>. Retrieved on: 10 June 2014.

PRIETO, V. G. **Chemigation.** Agricultura de las Americas, Overlnd Park, 1985.

RATTI, M.R.; PASSIG, F.H.. Characterisation of wastewater from the municipal slaughterhouse in the city of Mamborê/ PR. **Proceedings of the 24th Brazilian Congress of Sanitary and Environmental Engineering**. 02-07 September 2007 - Belo Horizonte /M. II - 258.

RAPOSO, J. R. **Sprinkler irrigation**. Lisbon: Clássica, 1979. 339 p.

CONAMA Resolution No. 430/2011 - "Establishes conditions and standards for the discharge of wastewater, supplements and amends Resolution No. 357 of 17 March 2005 of the National Environmental Council - CONAMA". DATE OF LEGISLATION: 13/05/2011 - Publication DOU N° 92, of 16/05/2011.

RODRIGUEZ, I.R.; MILLER, G.L.; McCARTY, B. Sprigged bermudagrass needs plenty of phosphorus at grow-in. *Golf Course Management,* 2000, p.59-62

SPERLING, Marcos von. **Stabilisation ponds. Basics of biological wastewater treatment**. UFMG Publishing House. Belo Horizonte: 1996.

THREADGILL, E. D. **Chernigation via sprinkler irrigation: current status and future developmentrnent**. Applied Engineering in Agriculture, St Joseph, 1985.

TURNER, T.R. *Turfgrass.* In: BENNETT, W.F. (ed.) Nutrient deficiencies and toxicities incrop plants. Texas Tech University, APS Press, Lubbock, TE, 1993, p187- 198.

VERGARA, Sylvia Constant. **Research projects and reports in administration**. 12th edition. São Paulo: Atlas, 2010.

WRI (Word Resources Institute). **World Resources 2002-2004 - Choices for the Earth**: Balance, Voice and Power. Washington DC, 2003.

Vonpar

SOLICITAÇÃO DE TRABALHO ACADÊMICO

DADOS GERAIS

NOME COLABORADOR:	PRISCILA PAULA LOPES MARTINS			MATRÍCULA	343050
EMAIL:	pmartins@vonpar.com.br				
CARGO / FUNÇÃO:	AUXILIAR ADMINISTRATIVA			CELULAR:	(55) 9969-4597
ÁREA:	MEIO AMBIENTE	RAMAL:	6514	DATA ADMISSÃO:	16/07/2013

DADOS DO TRABALHO

TÍTULO DO TRABALHO:	ESTUDO DA VIABILIDADE DA UTILIZAÇÃO DO EFLUENTE LÍQUIDO INDUSTRIAL PARA FERTIRRIGAÇÃO		
INSTITUIÇÃO DE ENSINO:	URI - UNIVERSIDADE REGIONAL INTEGRADA DO ALTO U	CURSO:	PÓS-GRADUAÇÃO EM LICENCIAMENTO AMBIENTAL
OBJETIVOS:	Este trabalho tem como objetivo verificar a viabilidade do reuso da água do efluente tratado da fábrica para fertirrigação.		

TÓPICOS / ASSUNTOS A SEREM ABORDADOS

Sistema de Gestão Ambiental; A Necessidade do Reúso de Água; Legistação; Efluente Indústrial; Fertirrigação; Parâmetros da Qualidade da Água; Descrição do Funcionamento da Estação de Tratamento de Efluente.

INFORMAÇÕES NECESSÁRIAS (FAVOR DESCREVER AS INFORMAÇÕES E QUAIS ÁREAS ENVOLVIDAS. UTILIZE FOLHAS EM ANEXO, SE NECESSÁRIO)

Preciso dos resultados dos parâmetros de 2012 e 2013: DQO, fósforo total, nitrogênio total kjeldahl, ph e sólidos sedimentais.

ORIENTADOR VONPAR: OBS.: O seu orientador será o seu Gestor.	Avelino Varisco	CARGO:	Gerente Indústrial	ÁREA:	Indústrial
DIAS E HORÁRIOS DE ACOMPANHAMENTO E SUPERVISÃO					
DATA DE ENTREGA DO TRABALHO:	01/10/2014	DATA DE APRESENTAÇÃO:	07/10/2014		

	SIM	NÃO		ABERTA	FECHADA
APRESENTAÇÃO COM BANCA ?	X		SE SIM, BANCA ABERTA OU FECHADA ?		X
JÁ REALIZOU TRABALHOS ANTERIORES NA VONPAR ?		X	SE SIM QUAL ASSUNTO ?		
			DATA REALIZAÇÃO:		

DECLARO QUE AS INFORMAÇÕES AQUI CONSIGNADAS SÃO VERDADEIRAS E COMPLETAS.

PORTO ALEGRE, ____/____/____

Priscila P L Martins
ASSINATURA DO COLABORADOR

AVELINO CARLOS VARISCO
Gerente Industrial
Matrícula 500081-5
ASSINATURA DO GESTOR

PARECER DO COMITÊ DE AVALIAÇÃO: (ÁREA RESERVADA A APROVAÇÃO E OBSERVAÇÕES DO COMITÊ)

Rogério [illegible] de Oliveira
Diretor de Finanças e TI

[illegible] Schaurich

Lúcio Cintra Soares
Diretor Jurídico

☐ APROVADO	REPROVADO	DATA:	VISTO UNIVERSIDADE VONPAR

Anexo 01 - Solicitação de Trabalho Acadêmico
NG-MTZ-DVP-004/1 TRABALHOS ACADÊMICOS

TABLE OF CONTENTS

More Books!

yes

I want morebooks!

Buy your books fast and straightforward online - at one of world's fastest growing online book stores! Environmentally sound due to Print-on-Demand technologies.

Buy your books online at
www.morebooks.shop

Kaufen Sie Ihre Bücher schnell und unkompliziert online – auf einer der am schnellsten wachsenden Buchhandelsplattformen weltweit! Dank Print-On-Demand umwelt- und ressourcenschonend produzi ert.

Bücher schneller online kaufen
www.morebooks.shop

info@omniscriptum.com
www.omniscriptum.com

OMNIScriptum

MIX
Papier aus verantwortungsvollen Quellen
Paper from responsible sources
FSC® C105338

Printed by Books on Demand GmbH, Norderstedt / Germany